# Cricut explore air 2

The Ultimate Guide to Discovering How to Make the Best Out
of your Cricut Explore Air 2 Model

CASSANDRA GIBBS

utter responsibility of the recipient reader. Under no circumstances will any legal responsibility or blame be held against the publisher for any reparation, damages, or monetary loss due to the information herein, either directly or indirectly.

Respective authors own all copyrights not held by the publisher.

The information herein is offered for informational purposes solely, and is universal as so. The presentation of the information is without contract or any type of guarantee assurance.

The trademarks that are used are without any consent, and the publication of the trademark is without permission or backing by the trademark owner. All trademarks and brands within this book are for clarifying purposes only and are the owned by the owners themselves, not affiliated with this document.

# TABLE OF CONTENTS

# INTRODUCTION

L et me start by thanking you for getting this book. Cricut Explore Air 2 is a great new machine. It is also a much-awaited machine that is replacing the original Cricut Explore Air.

In the case of this Cricut Explore Air 2, there are several changes that have been made. For starters, its speed has increased from 3,000 cuts per minute to 4,500 cuts per minute and it now weighs 50% less than the previous version of this Cricut Explore Air 2. It is also now water-resistant and comes with an automatic shutoff feature in case it gets damaged while being used by accident.

The Cricut Explore Air 2 is boundless for scrapbooking and card making enthusiasts. It comprises of a wide range of creative features that are helpful in creating great projects. It also comes with features that help avid crafters to save time and money. In addition, this machine has a user-friendly interface and great cutting capability.

It is also ideal for knowing your hobby well. These features of the Cricut Explore Air 2 are:

What you essentially need to know with this new machine?

The Cricut Explore Air 2 is the latest member of the Cricut family. This is a revolutionary machine that offers a wide range of cutting and crafting options. The user interface of the machine is easy to learn and use.

What does it come with?

This Cricut Explore Air 2 comes with an 8x8in cutting mat that is easy to store in a pocket and equally easy to mount on the machine. The iron and included USB cable are simple to use. This machine also has heavy duty motor that works at a speed of 3,000 cuts per minute, which enables it to cut through cardstock material easily. This means you can make custom cards, scrapbook pages, or other items effortlessly, without wasting time on things such as loading paper or struggling with low-quality papers. Also included is a pen which can be used for marking your project's placement before you start creating it.

What's new with this machine?

Cricut is known for spending more time on designing and making the machines that are much needed by the users. From the Cricut Explore Air 2 onwards, they have come up with machines that are much needed and useful. For instance, this Cricut Explore Air 2 has a magnetic strip on the side of the machine, which can be used to hold down ironing boards when they are not in use. This strengthens its functionality as an iron and helps you save some space while storing your ironing board when it is not being used.

The second thing they did was to put in a powerful motor that can cut even heavier materials easily and quickly. Also, one of the other things that is new to this machine is a mini cartridge it comes with that lets you get 12x12in projects done quickly without waiting for them to cut through several sheets of material multiple times. This means you do not have to reload your cartridge every time you want to make another project, which helps save precious time while creating your desired projects.

The machine is also more open and clearer than its predecessors. For example, a new design means that the machine has a space for storing two cartridges in order to be able to cut through bigger projects more quickly. Another addition is the smart guide that helps you place your project on the cutting mat while you're cutting. Basically, it tells you where your products are placed and how much space they occupy on the surface, which allows you to place them closer to where they should be.

Now, these are just few things about Cricut Explore Air 2. Let us learn more.

# THE CRICUT EXPLORE AIR 2

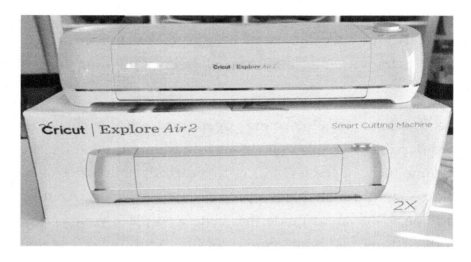

The Cricut Explore Air 2 can be regarded as an electronic cutter or a personal crafting machine which can be used in the cutting of different materials such as the cardstock, vinyl, Faux leather, Magnet sheets, sticker paper, Vellum, Fabric, Sticker Paper, etc.

The Cricut Explore Air 2 can make use of the pen and markers in writing, drawing as well as scoring your project with a nifty score tool. The machine can also be used in printing and cutting, as well.

The Cricut Explore Air 2 is an electronic cutting machine that makes use of a precise blade as well as series of rollers in cutting out images, just anything you can imagine. It is used in cutting out fancy paper shapes as well as fonts that came on cartridges.

The Cricut Explore Air has evolved, and now instead of making use of the cartridges, they have a library of cut files.

## Unboxing the Cricut Explore Air 2 Machine

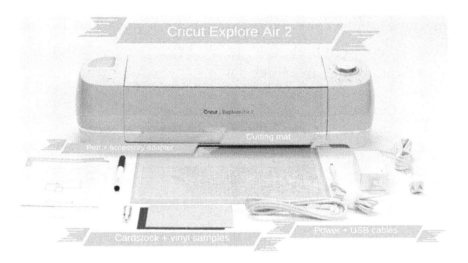

After purchasing the Cricut Explore Air 2 machine, it is essential to make sure it has all its accessories completely boxed in, and nothing is missing. If you find anything missing, you are advised to return it to where it was purchased or simply contact the Cricut support and inform them about the missing accessories. A complete packaged Cricut Explore Air 2 machine should have the following items in it:

- Cricut Explore Air 2
- Instruction manual
- Cricut cutting mat
- Cutting blade
- Silver pen and the accessory adapter

- Power and the USB cords
- The Cardstock and the Vinyl samples

It is to be noted that we have different kinds available, and depending on the kits you purchased, your Cricut Explore Air 2 machine might come with extra items included in it. The following are different kind of packages available for the Cricut Explore Air 2 machine:

- Ultimate Kit
- Tools Kit
- Vinyl starter Kit
- Complete Starter Kit
- The Premium Vinyl

## Characteristics of the Cricut Explore Air 2 Machine

- The Cricut Explore Air 2 machine is a wireless design and cut system kind of device.
- It can cut different varieties of materials easily because it has the Smart set dial.
- Cricut Explore Air 2 machine is a fast mode machine that enables it to cut and write twice as fast according to the settings of the tools and the images you are cutting.
- To make effective use of the Fast Mode, you are advised to select the Fast Mode in the design space and set the material between Vinyl and Cardstock.

- Accessories such as the blade, blade housing as well as the accessory adapter are all pre-installed in the Cricut Explore Air 2 machine.
- You will find settings of most common materials displayed on the dial, and there is an entire library of materials present in the Design space. You are advised to set the dial to custom.
- The Cricut Explore Air 2 machine has adequate storage, which makes everything you need readily available in it.
- The Cricut Explore Air 2 machine is an automated machine that enables it to adjust the Smart Set dials for the user.
- It is also having a cup which helps in holding your tools and also has two accessory compartments, which are the small and large compartments.
- The smaller compartment has magnetic strips that help in holding additional housings and the accessory adapter.
- The larger compartment helps in the storage of different Cricut tools.
- The Cricut Explore Air 2 machine is made up of the cartridge ports. The cartridge helps in linking your cartridges to your Cricut account online, which, in turn, helps you to access your images from any devices.

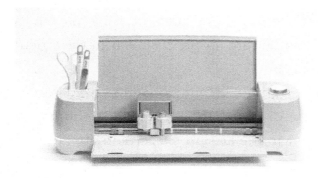

## Useful Tips

Once you go through this process of getting your machine setup, the machine will be registered automatically.

In a situation where you couldn't go through with the setup when the Cricut was connected to your PC at first, you will need to get the machine reconnected and visit the design portal on the Cricut website, or visit the Design Space Account menu, select New Machine Setup and follow the on-screen instructions that come up.

## Basic Set of The Cricut Tools Kit

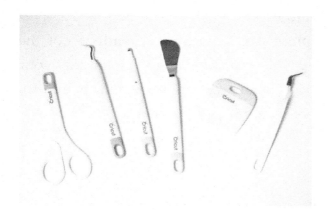

The tools should be packaged with the Cricut Explore Air 2 on purchase, and you can also get to buy them from Cricut directly or Amazon. It is sold for around $15 when purchased as a set. The craft tools set comprises of the following items;

**Tweezers**

This is designed in such a way that the handle can be squeezed open and also released to close. It is used in holding objects together while drying amongst other uses.

**Scraper**

The scraper is used in clearing the cutting mat and also works with vinyl.

**Scissors**

This is used as the name implies; to cut.

**Spatula**

The spatula helps in the careful lifting of materials off the cutting mat.

**Weeder**

The weeder is used in the removal of tiny little cuts or removing the vinyl from its liner.

## Finding the Machine Serial Number

You will find the serial number of the Cricut machine on the underside tag of the machine. It is directly below the barcode for older machines. The serial number is composed of the following:

A 12-character alphanumeric code

It begins with the following letters:

-Explore: E

-Explore Air: A

-Explore One: 1

-Explore Air 2: S

-Maker: Q

Model Numbers of the Cricut Machines

| Machine | Model Number |
| --- | --- |
| Explore One | CXLP101 |
| Explore Air | CXLP201 |
| Explore Air 2 | CXLP202 |
| Maker | CXLP301 |
| Explore | CXLP001 |
| Mini | CMN1001 |
| Gypsy | GPSY0001 |
| Cake Mini | CCM001 |
| Imagine | CRIM0001 |
| Expression | CREX001 |
| Expression 2 | CREX002 |
| Create | CRV2001 |
| Personal/VI | CRV001 |

# The Difference Between the Cricut Maker and Cricut Explore Air 2

It is made up of the Rotary blade, which is mostly used for cutting fabrics. It is also used in cutting leather, silk, and other materials.

In the Maker, the scoring pen is replaced by the scoring wheel, which has more delicate scored lines and sharper.

The Maker is made up of the knife blade used for thick and heavy materials such as the balsa wood and heavy chipboard.

It is made up of the Digital sewing pattern library, which provides access to hundreds of fabrics plans for an instant cut.

It can cut hundreds of more materials ranging from the finest paper to heavy fabrics.

Unlike the Explore Air 2, the Maker comes without the dial. The Maker is also made up of a ridge that is used for placing your tablet devices as well as redesigned storage areas.

Cricut Explore Air 2

In terms of cost, the Cricut Explore Air 2 offers the best value for money. It has lots of great features despite costing up to half of the price of the Maker.

It can be used for a diversity of projects such as the patterned vinyl t-shirt, reverse canvas project, vinyl on glass water bottles, craft cutting, etc.

## The Difference Between the Explore Air 2 And the Explore Air

Both the Explore Air 2, as well as the Maker, can cut, score, and write twice faster than the Explore Air can. Unlike the Explore Air that comes in the blue color, the Explore Air 2 does come in pastel colors. Irrespective of their differences, they are similar in some areas:

Air and Air 2 are both made up of a dual carriage that allows cutting and writing without having to change any tools.

Another notable similarity between these machines is that they both work with the deep cut blades and fine point.

## Cricut Access of the Cricut Explore Air 2 Machine

The premium access offered by the Cricut is called the Cricut Access, which gives you unlimited, though temporary, access to designs, and fonts. You can opt for purchasing your designs yourselves to have unhindered access anytime you need it.

Subscribing to Cricut Access

The Cricut Access gives you unlimited access to over one thousand projects as well as over thirty thousand images with over three hundred fonts. Therefore, to get the most of your Cricut machine, you are advised to subscribe to the Cricut Access, which will cost a monthly fee of just ten dollars.

By getting the Cricut Access, you will be saved the stress of having to worry about your expenses on a different project by saving you a lot of money buying at a flat rate.

## The Use of The Bluetooth In the Cricut Explore Air 2 Machine

The Cricut Explore Air 2 machine is designed to connect to your computer, iPad, or iPhone wirelessly though they can also be paired together as well.

Important Notes

The design space can be used with any image you wish to use it along with.

You are advised to always make a test cut first on a small amount of material to save you from messing up the whole project, which can be a result of incorrect settings calibration or messy blade.

The Cricut Explore Air 2 Machine, if paired with an iPhone, iPad, or an Android device, can be used without an internet connection.

# SETTING UP YOUR CRICUT EXPLORE AIR 2

Setting up your Cricut Explore Air 2 should be the next step after opening the box and unpacking its contents. It is vital that you set up the Cricut Explore Air 2 in a working space that is convenient for you. Consider the subsequent aspects when setting up your Cricut Explore Air 2

1.  Lighting

2.  Power source

3.  Workspace configuration

4.  Ergonomics

## Lighting:

It is crucial that where you set up your Cricut Explore Air 2 is well lit. This lets you see what you are doing with the machine and lets you set it and change accessories with ease. Lighting could be natural (that is from sunlight) or artificial from bulbs and lamps. Lighting is very important as it prevents you from straining your eyes.

## Power Source:

Since the Cricut Explore Air 2 is powered by electricity, a power outlet is important in setting it up. Set your Cricut

Explore Air 2 as close to a power outlet as the power cable permits. This prevents the issue of entangling cables that make workspace untidy that occur when extension cables are used.

## Work Space Configuration:

You will need to decide how you wish to configure your workspace before you set up your Cricut Explore Air 2. You need to decide where what needs to be kept. A good workspace configuration makes your craft making easy, convenient and enjoyable.

## Ergonomics:

Consider ergonomic factors as you set up your Cricut Explore Air 2. The Cricut Explore Air 2 set be set up on a work table that is at a convenient height for you. A work table that is too high or too low ends up being a source of back pain and strain.

## Linking the Cricut Explore Air 2 to Your Computer

The Cricut Explore Air 2 does not work by itself. To make the best out of it, you connect it to a computer. The Cricut Explore Air 2 works with PCs from Microsoft and Macs from Apple. Hooking up the Cricut Explore Air 2 to a computer is easy. Follow the steps below to get started

To get your Cricut Explore Air 2 working with a computer, you need to have Cricut Design Space installed and running on your computer.

Setting up the Cricut Explore Air 2 is easy! Use these steps and let's get started.

1.  Open the box and unpack the Cricut Explore Air 2 and the accessories.
2.  Place the Cricut Explore Air 2 on a flat work surface. Leave at least 10 inches of space behind the Cricut Explore Air 2. This is to allow the Cutting Mat roll forward and back conveniently behind the Cricut Explore Air 2 as the machine cuts the material.
3.  Push the "Open" button
4.  Carefully fix the accessory holder and the blades/blade housing in the tool holders.
5.  Connect the USB cord to the Cricut Explore Air 2 and connect it to your computer.
6.  Connect the power cord to the Cricut Explore Air 2 and plug it into a power outlet and switch on the power outlet.
7.  Switch on the Cricut Explore Air 2 machine.
8.  Your computer will detect the machine and install the drivers that are necessary.
9.  If you wish you can connect the Cricut Explore Air 2 to your PC or Mac computer using Bluetooth.
10. Launch your browser and go to design.Cricut.com/setup
11. Login or Create your Cricut ID

12. Download the Design Space Plugin
13. Follow onscreen instructions and install the plugin.
14. As soon as the installation is finished, computer will alert you to make a project.

## Linking the Cricut Explore Air 2 to your Mac via Bluetooth

1. Keep your Cricut Explore Air 2 within 10 feet of your Mac.

2. Go to Apple Menu and then select System Preferences.

3. Click the Bluetooth icon. Check to ensure the Bluetooth function is turned on.

4. Choose your Cricut Explore Air 2 from a list of available Bluetooth devices.

5. Click on Pair.

6. Use the code 0000 and select "pair".

Note that the Mac computer will only show connected when it is communicating with the Cricut Explore Air 2 during the cutting process.

## Linking the Cricut Explore Air 2 to your iPhone via Bluetooth

1. Keep your Cricut Explore Air 2 within 10 feet of your iPhone.

2. Go to Settings on your mobile device then select the Bluetooth option.

3. Switch on the Bluetooth if it is off.

4. Select the Cricut Explore Air 2 from the list of available Bluetooth devices.

5. Click on Pair.

6. Use the code 0000 and select "pair".

7. Your machine can now cut from your iPhone.

## Linking the Cricut Explore Air 2 to your Android device via Bluetooth

1. Keep your Cricut Explore Air 2 within 10 feet of your android device.

2. Go to Settings on your mobile phone then select the Bluetooth option.

3. Switch on the Bluetooth if it is off.

4. Select the Cricut Explore Air 2 from the list of available Bluetooth devices.

5. When prompted for a code, use the code 0000 and select pair.

6. Your machine can now cut from your android device.

## Linking the Cricut Explore Air 2 to your Windows Computer via Bluetooth

1. Keep your Cricut Explore Air 2 within 10 feet of your Windows computer.

2. Go to the Start Menu

3. Select settings

4. Select the devices option

5. Turn Bluetooth on and click on Add Bluetooth or Other Device

6. Select Bluetooth, the computer will sense the Cricut Explore Air 2 and show it in the list of available Bluetooth devices.

7. When asked for a pairing code, use 0000

8. Select Connect.

9. Your Cricut Explore Air 2 can now cut from your Windows Computer.

# Cricut Access

Cricut Access is something a lot of Cricut users don't understand. Hence a lot of misinformation flies around regarding it. The information I will provide here will help you decide whether you need it or not. Here is what you should about Cricut Access;

Cricut Access allows you to access thousands of images, fonts, and ready-made projects. All these come for a fee. Membership of Cricut Access comes in three major categories with different payment plans.

The perfect starter plans

This strategy is good for you if you just want to have a look before deciding whether you want to commit. It is a monthly plan and costs about $9.99

**Annual Plan**

This plan incorporates the benefits of the monthly plan. When you look at it closely, you'd realize you pay $7.99 per month – instead of $9.99. That means you pay upfront $95.88.

**Premium Plan**

The premium plan gives you all the profits of the other plans and also:

Up to 50% discounts on fonts, graphics, and ready-made projects.

Free economy shipping for purchases over $50.

Annually it costs $119.88. It would cost $9.99 monthly.

## What Sets Cricut Access And Cricut Design Space Apart?

Several people ask, what is the difference between Cricut Access with Cricut Design Space? The difference between both is very simple. Cricut Design Space is free software where you prepare your projects before sending them to your Cricut Explore Air to cut it. Think of it as a digital workshop you use to prepare your projects.

Cricut Access is a platform where you pay to get access to fonts, graphics, and readymade projects you can use in Cricut Design Space.

You can use Cricut Access images within Cricut Design Space. However, you will have to pay before sending them to be cut. You can pay as you go.

## Cartridges

What are Cricut Cartridges? Cricut cartridges are a library of images that users can buy to use in creating their projects on their Cricut machine. Usually, these cartridges collect images focusing on a season (e. g Christmas or Easter), characters, or concept. A certain common trait links all the content of a cartridge together.

The Cartridges are physical devices that you plug into your Cricut Explore Air. You plug the cartridge into the cartridge port.

Within Cricut Access there are lots of "Cricut cartridges". These cartridges are not physical cartridges; they are digital libraries just like the physical cartridges. Once you purchase a cartridge, you can use it even without a subscription to Cricut Access. You can use Cartridges from your older machine on your Cricut Explore Air. Once linked to your account, you can have access to the content of the cartridge without even the physical unit. With Cricut Access there is little need to get physical cartridges.

Linking Cartridges with the Cricut Explore Air

While you cannot use your machine offline, your cartridges will work fine. Here is how to link your cartridge with the Cricut Explore Air.

1. Using your browser, visit www.cricut.com/design and sign in to your account.
2. After logging in, click on the account button (it is green in color).
3. Click on "Cartridge Linking" from the drop-down menu.
4. Fix the cartridge firmly in the cartridge port. Ensure the machine is switched on and connected to the PC.
5. The cartridge if detected will trigger an alert prompting you to link the cartridge to your account.
6. Click "Link Cartridge"

# BEST TOOLS AND ACCESSORIES FOR CRICUT EXPLORE AIR 2

## Cutting Mat

The Cutting Mat gives a platform on how the materials are going to be laid into the Cricut Machine. It helps in getting the content securely placed by being sticky, holds on firmly to the article.

The cutting mat is designed to be sticky on one of the sides to securely hold the material in place during the cutting, scoring, or inking process.

The cutting mat is made up of three types, with each of them used for different kinds of materials. So, the kind of cutting mat you choose to use solely depends on the materials you are working with.

Here are the three types of Cutting mats as well as the materials that work with each of them:

- Standard Grip (the one in green color)
- Window clings
- Vinyl
- Regular with Embossed cardstock
- Heat transfer (Iron-on) with regular vinyl
- Firm Grip (the one in purple color)
- Magnetic material
- Foam
- Wood as well as Balsa
- Posterboard
- Backed fabric
- Corrugated Cardboard
- Leather with Suede
- Chipboard
- Light grip (blue color)
- Light cardstock
- Construction paper
- Printer with scrapbook paper

- Vellum
- De-tacking your Cutting Mat

It is to be noted that the Air 2 is made up of a green regulatory cutting mat while the Cricut Maker always comes with a shade of blue grip mat. Recall that materials are always placed on these mats before they are inserted into the machine.

The green cutting mat present in the Explore Air 2 is sticky when new. Therefore, it is advisable to put a clean, dry cotton material on top the mat to prime it after peeling the plastic cover off from your initial project.

It can be a hassle in getting the cardstock off even with all the tools available due to its stickiness. Thus, it is effortless to get the project damaged while trying to detach it. Nevertheless, the blue light grip mat should not give you this kind of problem. So, it is advisable to purchase this for your paper and card projects instead of having to de-tack the green mat.

## Cutting Mat Covers

The plastic shield is used for covering the cutting mat when purchased. The plastic shield can be pulled off and placed back quickly.

You are always advised to keep and place back the cover of the mat after you are done ever to keep the cloth clean and helps maintain the stickiness.

It is important to always wipe over your cutting mat with some baby wipes. In cleaning your cutting mat, the nonalcoholic baby wipes are recommended to keep your cutting mat from building up with vinyl and cardstock residue after cutting processes.

It also keeps it clean from specks of dust and lint that may be floating about.

## Tool Cup

The tool cup is the part that holds scissors, pens, and other Cricut tools in use. The pen is used by getting the accessory clamp A opened and dropping in the pen down into it, after which the clamp is then closed.

## Accessory Storage Compartments

Apart from the Tool Cup, the Cricut Explore Air 2 machine is made up of two compartments which are also used in holding tools, these are: - Smaller Compartment - Larger Compartment

The smaller compartment is positioned at the left for holding additional blade housings, the accessory adapter as well as the blades. The lower chamber is made up of a magnetic strip for securely keeping the replacement blades and prevents it from rolling.

The larger compartment is used to store more extended tools and pens.

## Accessory Clamp A

The accessory clamp A comes pre-installed as the accessory adapter, and the pen for drawing instead for having to cut can be inserted through this part. It also helps in holding the scoring blades.

## The Cricut Scoring Stylus

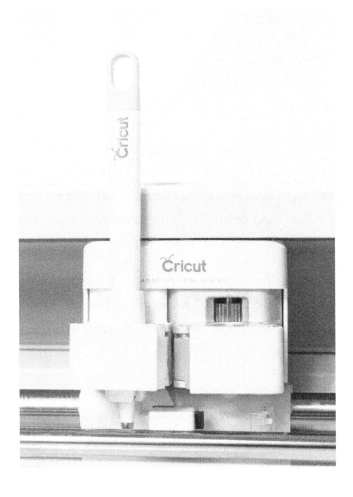

The Cricut Scoring Stylus is an essential tool, especially for your card projects. So, on purchase, it is necessary to check to make sure this tool comes with the Cricut machine.

They are available for free when you purchase the Cricut machine.

## Blade Clamp A

Cricut Explore Air Machine has the Blade clamp A already pre-installed in them. The replacement or the removal of bits of vinyl can also be done here.

## Smart Set Dial

The Cricut Explore Air machine, through its fast mode of operation, enables the user to turn and indicate which material is to be cut with the twice fast style with the use of the Smart Set dial. What you need to do is to interchange the Smart Set dial and choose the material you will be cutting.

Removing and Replacing the Accessory and the Blade clamps of the Cricut Explore Air Machine To remove the accessory clamp or blade, pull open the lever, after which you will then get the metal housing pulled out.

The blade is positioned seated inside; having a tiny plunger on the top, pressing this down will reveal the edge which is held out magnetically.

To get the blade replaced, if the need arises, all you have to do is to get the edge pulled out and drop the new knife in.

There are two significant features the Cricut Explore Air 2 offers which are absent in the Cricut Explore One. First of all, it is Bluetooth enabled, this means you are not limited by cable lengths when configuring your workspace. A significant snag with previous devices was the fact that they had to be connected to the computer with a USB cable hence the laptop had to be close to the machine.

Secondly, the Cricut Explore Air 2 has does not have just one tool holder. It has the capacity to work with two tools. With a secondary tool holder, you can carry out two different operations simultaneously. You can cut and write or score and cut at the same time. This saves a lot of time and makes your work very easy.

## Standard Grip Cutting Mat

The cutting mat is sticky in nature. It is made sticky so that it holds the material being cut in place as it is being cut. Before any operations are carried out, the material to be cut or written on is placed on the Cutting Mat. The mat serves as the work surface for the machine.

## Blade and Housing

This comes preinstalled in the machine. The blade and its housing are attached to one of the two tool holders. You can get other blades and blade holders to cut unique materials

## Cricut Cardstock

In the box, you have some cardstock. This lets you hit the ground in succession and begin your first project. The cardstock comes in different colors and textures. You could purchase extra material if the cardstock provided in the box proves to be inadequate.

## Pen and Accessory Adapter

The adapter is preinstalled on the second tool holder. It is on this tool holder that the pen or any other accessory is affixed. The adapter holds whatever accessory you wish to use on the secondary tool holder. To use a pen with it, you simply drop a pen into it.

## Power Cord

The Cricut Explore Air 2 runs on electricity. The power cord connects the machine to a power outlet.

## USB Cord

The USB cord connects the device to the computer. It is vital to compare the Cricut Explore Air 2 to the computer with the

USB cord when connecting for the first time. This lets the necessary drivers be installed in the networks. After the essential drivers get installed, subsequent connections can be made wirelessly.

## Mat Guides

The Mat Guides are found on the sides of the tray. They keep the Cutting Mat firmly in place and prevent it from moving as the material upon it is being cut. This helps achieve exact and intricate cuts.

## Storage Compartments

There are two storage compartments. Both compartments are found under the tray. The first compartment is used for storing blades and blade housing safely. The second compartment is used for the storage of other accessories like markers, pens, and their housing adapters.

## USB Port

This is where the USB cord is connected.

## Power Port

This is where the power cord goes in.

## Power Button

This button wakes up the Cricut Explore Air 2. It is also the button to push once you wish to shut down the machine.

Smart Set Dial

The smart set dial sets the machine to the type of material being cut. There are different materials pre-set, what you just do is to turn the dial to the preset content you wish to operate on. For instance, if you are working on Vinyl, you will simply turn the dial to "Vinyl"

## Load/Unload Mat/Go/Pause

These are three buttons found near the Smart Set Dial. There are used to control movements of the Cutting Mat.

The Load/Unload Mat button loads the Cutting Mat with materials to be operated on by the tools. When the button is pushed and equipment is already loaded, it rolls out the Cutting Mat so that the material can be removed.

The Go button starts an operation. After you have loaded material to a machine, you push the Go button to commence services.

The Pause button puts on holds any ongoing operation.

# Rollers

The rollers work to push the material being operated under the tool holders so that they can be worked on. The Cutting Mat is placed on the rollers and they roll back and forth to push the cutting mat back and forth. This was the tool holder can reach all parts of the material being worked on to give an exact cut.

Cricut Explore Air 2 Accessories

Accessory clamp A is the pre-installed accessory adapter where you insert your Cricut pen for drawing and used to hold scoring blades. To use a pen, simply open the accessory clamp A, push it down till you hear a click sound, then close the clamp.

Blade clamp B is also pre-installed with blades for cutting your materials and can be replaced when there is need to.

Tool cup is used to hold your scissors, pens, etc.

Smart Set dial used to select the material you intend to cut and which mode to use to reduce your content.

Accessory storage compartments (two in number: small and large). The lower chamber is on the left and has a magnetic strip which stores extra blades, blade housings, and accessory adapter to keep them safe and prevent them rolling around. The larger compartment serves to safeguards more extended pens/tools.

Cutting mat used to load your material into Cricut Explore Air 2. It is made sticky to hold your content firmly while it is being worked on by Cricut Explore Air 2 machine. There are four Cricut cutting mat at the moment including Standard Grip, Fabric Grip, LightGrip, and Strong Grip cutting mats. Their applications are different just like their names.

# BASIC PROCEDURES

## Print and Cut with Cricut Explore Air 2

The Cricut Explore Air 2 comes with Print Then Cut features. With this, you can print out your images using your inkjet home printers and have your Cricut Explore cut them out with perfect precision. Say goodbye to inaccuracies caused by scissors!

## Prepare Images for Printing

To make an image printable, you have to convert it to Linetype. This works on all images. You can also use the Flatten tool from Layers Panel to convert multiple layers for joint Printing.

Cricut library is filled with predesigned images that are ready to print. They appear on the design screen, where you can directly print and cut them. They are pre-aligned in the Layers panel as a single layer. They also possess a Print Linetype, which indicates that the image will be printed on your home computer and then cut using your Cricut Explore Air 2.

To locate Printables, click on the Filters icon and check the box marked Printables. Select your preferred image. A printer icon should be displayed on the image title. Include it to your canvas and click on "Make it to Print Then Cut."

# Print Then Cut Projects

After you have included printable images to your project, or switched the image Linetype to Print, click on "Make it" from Design Space. The preview image will be displayed, with a cut censor marking. Click on Continue to proceed to the cut interface.

The next screen comes up, where you will select your device from the drop-down menu. Click on Send to Printer to open the Print Then Cut interaction.

The images will be fitted with an image bleed, which will remove the white border from the cut image.

Utilize your Home Printer to print out the page. After, fix the paper on the Cricut cutting mat, and fix it in the Cricut machine. Your Explore Air 2 scans the sensor marking and accurately cut around the image.

Print Then Cut has a maximum image size of 9.25" × 6.75". The default material is 8.5" × 11". This is a permanent measure.

*Consequential:* Interference may be caused by colored materials, reflective materials, or materials with any pattern at all. The sensors might not be able to detect the cut sensor marks. You should use an Inkjet printer and 8.5" × 11" white materials for all your Print Then Cut processes with Cricut Explore. However, the Cricut Maker can Print Then Cut on light to medium-colored papers.

## Things to Remember

*Print Then Cut all in one session:* To avoid error, you can best carry out the entire Print Then Cut process in the same browser and on the same computer. It is ok to save your Print Then Cut projects for another time within the Design Space. However, you should not change browsers or computers during an ongoing print and cut. Also, you shouldn't save a Print Then Cut image as a PDF and print it outside the Design Space flow. This could result in incorrect sizing cut or sensor marks. To prevent all this, Print Then Cut your projects in one Design Space session.

*Image Bleed:* A bleed is a small border that surrounds each image to ease the cutting. This Bleed is assigned automatically to each image. You can turn it on or off from the Project Preview screen. The Bleed makes the image appear distorted or fuzzy; however, the border will be trimmed entirely off when cutting. I recommend you leave it ON.

*Proper Material Placement on Cutting Mat:* First, straighten up your material and clear out all wrinkles. This way, the machine can adequately detect the cut sensor marks surrounding your image. Then your printable material must be placed at the top left corner of the cutting mat, perfectly aligned with the top-left edge of the adhesive cutting mat. If you use a standard printer or copy paper, you should use the Cricut LightGrip mat.

# Print Then Cut Troubleshooting

*Print Then Cut Calibration:* These are a series of superficial cuts, questions, and answers, specially made to aid your Cricut in cutting precisely along the edge of your printed image.

*Explore is not reading sensor marks:* Visit the Cricut website to find out more about this and how to clear it.

*Note:* To use Print Then Cut with an iOS device, the printer must be equipped with AirPrint. You can find out more about this on the Apple help site.

*Significant:* The Print Then Cut feature is NOT available on Android.

# Stamp Basic Shapes on Cricut Explore Air 2

Cricut Design Space comes with a "basic shapes" feature in its Design Panel. The shapes contained therein are available to you, free of charge. You can easily add circles, triangles, rectangles, hearts, and so on, using them as the base for your projects.

Basic Shapes Screenshot

You can create a card front in Design Space. Simply go to the Shape section and insert a square shape. Adjust the size to 4.25" × 5.5". If you wish to cut an entire card base, insert a square and size it to 8.5" × 5.5".

Add Cut Lines and Score Lines

Shapes inserted into the canvas usually have a definite cut line. However, after adding an image, a dashed line is added to it. So, after inserting your shape, you insert your desired image, and the dashed line appears, which you can adjust to set how it is cut.

Score Screenshot

This is a scoreline. Your machine is set to cut and score the envelope for you; all you need is a scoring tool. You can switch lines to cut, draw, or score. If you are not certain of the type of lines a shape has, look into the Layers panel. There you'll find which ones to score or cut. You can also use the Edit bar to change the line type of a shape.

Card Base Screenshot

Complete your card Base by inserting a scoreline. These Score lines can also be inserted from the same Shapes section of the Design panel. Adjust your Score line to 5.5", drag it to the card base, and select the two images under Align. In the Edit bar, select Center. The scoreline is then perfectly centered. With both the line and card base still selected, click Attach in the Layers panel. Use Attach to keep your scoreline in the same position, even if the shape is moved on the canvas.

## Using the Slice Tool

The Slice Tool can be used to make sentiments for your cards. You can find the Slice Tool from the functions at the bottom of the Layers Panel, right by the Weld and Contour. With the Slice Tool, you can cut the text or an image out of another shape. Just fix your image or word on top of the one you want to cut. Select the two shapes, then click Slice in the Layers Panel.

Slice Screenshot

This tool can be used to duplicate shapes. After use, click on the image you cut out. You'll get the shape itself and the shape you cut out of the background.

Use Stencils to Paint on Fabric

When designing for stencils, an important point to remember is to think about the negative space you are creating and how to keep the positive space intact. An excellent way to start is with a graphic of any kind, like an illustration, letters, or a whole design. You should also make a cutout for the Cricut that stays together. The last thing you want is a floating element or piece from your design.

Making a Letter Stencil Using Cricut

Letter stencils are arguably the hardest to make on Cricut. This is because it exhibits the floating design pieces more often than any other Stencils. However, there's a quick, easy fix to it. You can highlight the rectangle silver technique to slice your enclosed letters at their tiniest parts.

# Top Stencil Fonts on Cricut

There are quite a number of Cricut fonts to choose from in the Design Space. These fonts do not possess floating elements. Some great options include:

- Doodle Type
- Dinosaur Tracks
- 3 Birds in paradise
- Girly Stencil
- Blippo Come Stencil
- Wednesday Stencil
- Cricut Alphabet-Circle
- Don Juan
- Glaser Stencil

## Stencil Materials for Cutting Machines

Many diverse materials can be used to make Stencils, such as vinyl, paper, plastic, etc. Your decision may depend on the blank materials, the paint you intend on using, or your imagined design.

Top Materials for Reusable Stencils

If you're making use of a finite medium, you should make reusable Stencils. This is to ensure you do not waste materials.

However, you should note that if your design contains floating materials, you might have to resort to using a silkscreen. Some reusable stencil materials include:

- Mylar Sheets

- Stencil Roll Film

- Laminating Sheets

Top Materials for Cooking Related Stencils

Not all Stencils are food-grade materials. It is essential to know the ones you can use for your foods, not to endanger your health. Some top stencils include:

- Wax Paper

- Parchment Paper

- Grafix Clear Sheets

Top Disposable Stencil Materials

When stenciling with fabric, it is best to use a disposable material due to the paint's nature to avoid getting stains everywhere. These materials are sticky, making it much easier to operate with floating elements in your design. Some of them include:

- Transfer Paper

- Contact Paper

- Removable vinyl

Making Reusable Stencils with Cricut Explore Air 2

The recommendation for reusable stencils is to make use of Mylar Plastic sheets. They are straightforward to use and are very stable. Not to mention, very easy to wash.

## Cricut Settings for Contact Paper

Contact paper sounds great, but is, in fact, considerably weak, which causes it to snag. It is advisable that you only set it on vinyl less for your Stencils. It might cut through, but it doesn't matter, as long as it is only used for stencils. You could also use a blue light pen for a more uncomplicated peel.

## Making a Stencil for Painting with Cricut

There are several available surfaces to paint with a stencil. With the Cricut, you can make Stencils from the most popular materials. Among these materials are wood, canvas, fabric, ceramics, and chalkboard.

Adhesive stencils work best with painting. No matter how viscous your painting is, it will most likely run or bleed with a non-adhesive stencil. It is better to use adhesive stencil materials when painting, such as contact paper, sticky laminating sheets, removable vinyl, and transfer paper.

As for porous medium such as wood, you should use a mid podge to seal the cutout edges before painting. Just smear a layer of mod Lodge on the part that's been cut out of the wood.

You could also make use of a sponge or sponge brush when painting with stencils.

How Long Should Paint Be Left to Dry Before Removing the Stencil

Leave the paint until it is dry to the touch. It is best to peel it off after it has dried. This is to avoid smearing wet paint all over your work and yourself. If the base material is stretchy, you risk stretching the whole design in an ugly way when you peel off the paint wet. It's really not that complicated, so don't stress over it. Just peel when dry.

# CUTTING HEAVY AND LIGHT MATERIALS

Calibration makes it easy for you to use a blade when you want to use it for the first time. It is necessary that you complete the calibration because it helps the Cricut machine recognize the type of blade housing you wish to use. The calibration is done in the blade housing that contains the blade. So anytime you feel like replacing a blade, you don't need to do calibrate the machine again because it has already been calibrated. The only reason you should recalibrate the blade housing is if you want to use a different blade housing in the machine. Otherwise, there will be no need for recalibration.

## How to Calibrate Your Cricut Air 2?

We will be starting with how to calibrate the knife blade before forging ahead on other calibration.

Put a white piece of printing paper on the cutting mat.

Align it and select continue.

A menu will drop down. Select the machine in use.

An option will tell you to insert your mat by means of the printed paper into the machine with the load/unload button. Select load.

After you are done, select, "Go" to begin calibration.

Your Cricut Explore Air 2 will cut seven sets of lines that overlap in the middle. Remove the mat from the machine. With caution, determine which cut has the best overlap.

The best cuts usually appear as a single cut. Once you have made your selection, select, "Continue" from the drop-down menu.

## How to Calibrate Your Printer for Print Then Cut

Print then Cut is a feature that's found in the Cricut Design Space. Calibrating your printer will allow it to print and then, cut the image with better precision. Without print then cut calibration, your Cricut Explore will not exactly cut your printed images well.

If you must be using the Print then Cut feature on your Cricut Explore Air 2 for the first time, you will have to calibrate it. Most Cricut Explore Air 2 comes pre-calibrated. However, if yours did not come calibrated, follow the steps below to set up your Print then Cut calibration.

Select, "Calibration" from the Account drop-down menu. Confirm you have signed in with the correct specifics.

You will see, "Start Calibration" with a note and a green button with, "Continue" by the end of the right-hand side of the screen. Select the green button.

Load any measurement of a white paper material into your printer as a calibration sheet. Don't load colored materials as it will hinder your Cricut from reading the cut sensor or marks correctly.

Click, "Continue".

A print dialogue box will appear. Confirm if the destination is your printer and click, "Print".

Now, connect your Cricut Explore Air 2 to a computer. You can use either Mac or Windows. Ensure your Cricut is powered on.

Once the Explore Air 2 has been detected, place the calibration sheet on the cutting mat. Follow the instructions on the screen carefully.

Load the calibration sheet into your Cricut Explore Air 2 and turn the smart set dial to the paper setting.

Select "Go" on your Cricut.

You will see the cut sensor marks around your images. Make a test cut around the little center square in the middle.

Once it is done cutting, observe the nature of the cutting. Notice the small cut lines around the small square at the center. If the cut lines went around the printed line in a similar fashion, select "Yes" and then "Continue".

Your Cricut Explore Air 2 will make some vertical and some horizontal cuts on the calibration sheet. When your Cricut is done cutting, observe again, the lines around the print page. Which cuts are closest to the print line?

After you have selected the corresponding numbers in the menu, select, "Continue".

Your Cricut will cut the bigger rectangle. When it is done cutting, observe the precision of the cut line. If satisfactory, select "Yes" followed by "Continue". Otherwise, select "No" and then "Continue".

Select "Save and close".

## How to Calibrate A Rotary Blade

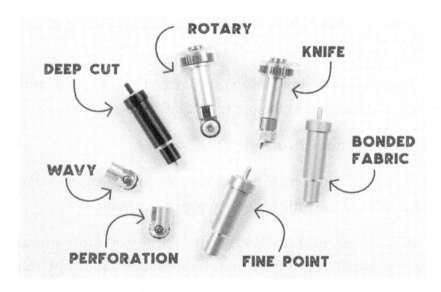

Each time you change a rotary blade, it is important you perform a rotary blade calibration always to enhance precise cutting. It is worthy to note that the Cricut rotary blade is exclusive to Cricut maker only. That's because the Cricut

Explore Air 2 lacks an Adaptive Tool System to control how the blade is used. However, we are talking about Cricut calibration so, it is fair we talk about rotary blade calibration for users that have other Cricut machines.

Calibrating the rotary blade is simple and similar to that of a knife blade. To calibrate the rotary blade:

Click open Design Space on your Mac/Windows PC.

Select "Menu" and click "Calibration". You must have inserted your rotary blade housing. Remember to insert your knife blade into clamp "B".

Select, "Rotary blade" among the three calibration options.

Put a white piece of printing paper on the cutting mat. Align it and select continue.

A menu will drop down. Select the machine in use.

An option will tell you to insert your mat with the printed paper into the machine with the load/unload button. Select load.

After you have done so, select, "Go" to begin calibration.

Congratulations! Your knife blade calibration is complete.

A rotary blade can cut the following fabrics without any hindrance;

- Canvas
- Cashmere

- Cotton
- Faux leather
- Fleece
- Linen
- Velvet
- Silk
- Polyester

# FAQS ABOUT CRICUT EXPLORE AIR 2

## Why Does Design Space Say My Cricut Machine Is in Use When It's Not?

To resolve this, make sure that you've completed the New Machine Setup for your Cricut. Try Design Space in another browser. The two that work best are Google Chrome and Mozilla Firefox; if it doesn't work in one of those, try the other. If that doesn't clear the error, try a different USB port and USB cable. Detach the machine from the computer then turn it off. While it's off, restart your computer. After your computer restarts, reconnect the machine and turn it on. Wait a few moments, then try Design Space again. If you're still having the same problem, contact Cricut Member Care.

## Why Doesn't My Cut Match the Preview in Design Space?

Test another image and see if the same thing happens. If it's only happening with the one project, create a new project and start over or try a different image. If it happens with a second project, and your machine is connected with Bluetooth, disconnect that and plug it in by means of a USB cable. Larger projects may sometimes have difficulty communicating the cuts over Bluetooth. If you can't connect with USB or the problem is still occurring, check that your computer matches or exceeds the system requirements for running Design Space. If it doesn't, try the project on a different computer or mobile device that does. If your computer does meet the requirements, open Design Space in a different browser and try again. If the problem lingers, try a changed USB cable. Finally, if the issue still hasn't resolved, contact Cricut Member Care.

## How to Install USB Drivers for My Cricut Machine?

Typically, the Cricut drivers are automatically installed when you connect it with a USB cable. If Design Space doesn't see your machine, you can try this to troubleshoot the driver installation. First, open Device Manager on your computer. You'll need to have administrator rights. For Windows 7, click Start, right-click on Computer, and select Manage. For Windows 8 and up, right-click on the Start icon and click Computer Management. Within Computer Management, click Device Manager on the left-hand side. Find your Cricut machine on the list—it should be listed under Ports. Still, it might be under Other Devices or Universal Serial Bus Controllers. Right-click on it and select Update Driver Software. When a box that pops up, choose Browse My Computer. In the box on the next screen, type in %APPDATA% and click Browse. Extra box will pop up where you can search through folders. Find AppData and expand it. Click Roaming, then CricutDesignSpace, then Web, then

Drivers, then CricutDrivers, and click OK. Click Next to install these drivers. Once it's finished, restart your computer. Once it's on, open Design Space again to see if it recognizes your machine.

## Is Wireless Bluetooth Adapter Required for All Cricut Explore Machines?

No. It is only required for Explore and Explore One. Explore Air and Explore Air 2 have in-built Bluetooth and therefore no need for Wireless Bluetooth Adapter.

## How Do You Differentiate Between the Cricut Explore Machines?

The tool holder is the first difference. Explore One has one tool holder which means it can cut & score in two steps while Explore, Explore Air, and Explore Air 2 come with double tool holder for cut & write or cut & score in one single step.

Explore and Explore One require a Cricut Wireless Bluetooth Adapter to cut wirelessly from your iOS, Android or computer while Explore Air and Explore Air 2 have in-built Bluetooth.

## Is Carry Bag Included in Explore Series Machine Package?

No. carry bag is not included in the package, but you can buy it separately.

## Is It Possible to Write & Score with My Explore One Machine?

Yes, but to do this, you will need to buy Explore One Accessory Adapter. Switch this adapter with the blade housing to write or score with Explore One machine.

## Are the Weights and Dimensions of Explore Series Machine Similar?

Yes, they are similar. The approximate weight is 9.5 kg (21 lbs.), length: 56.33cm (22.17"), width: 17.76cm (6.99") and height: 15.16cm (5.97").

## Why Is My Cricut Machine Making A Grinding Noise?

If it's the carriage car making a loud noise after you press the cut button, and it sounds like the carriage might be hitting the side of the machine, record a short video of it and send it to Cricut Member Care. If the noise is coming from a brand-new engine the first time you use it, contact Cricut Member Care. Otherwise, make sure that you're using the original power cord that came with your device. If the machine isn't getting the correct voltage, it may produce a grinding sound. If you are using the machine's power cord, adjust your pressure settings. If it's too high, it might have an unusual sound. Decrease it in increments of 2–4, and do some test cuts. If it's still making the issue even after decreasing the cutting pressure, contact Cricut Member Care.

## What If My Cricut Is Making A Different Loud Noise?

Make sure that you don't have Fast Mode engaged for cutting or writing. If it's not on, take a short video of the problem to send to Cricut Member Care.

## Why Is My Mat Going into The Machine Crooked?

Check the roller bar to see if it's loose, damaged, or uneven. If it is, take a photo or video of it to send to Cricut Member Care. If the roller bar seems fine, make sure that you're using the right mat size for the machine. Next, make sure the mat is correctly lined up with the guides and that the edge is underneath the roller bar when you prepare to load it. If it's still loading crookedly even when properly lined up with the guides, try applying gentle pressure to the mat to get it under the roller bar once it starts. If none of this works, contact Cricut Member Care.

## Why Isn't the Smart Set Dial Changing the Material in Design Space?

Make sure that the USB cable between the computer and the Cricut Explore is appropriately connected. If so, disconnect the Explorer from the computer and turn it off. Restart your computer. Once it's on, turn on the Explore, plug it into the computer, and try the cut again. If it still isn't changing the material, connect the USB cable to a different port on the computer. If it's still not working, try Design Space in multiple web browsers and see if the problem replicates. If it does, try an entirely different USB cable. Check for Firmware Updates for the Explore. If you don't have another USB cable, the Firmware Update doesn't help, or there are no Firmware Updates, contact Cricut Member Care.

## What Do I Do If My Cricut Maker Stopped Partway Through A Cut?

If the Knife Blade stops cutting and the Go button is flashing, the Maker has encountered some sort of error. In Design Space, you'll get a notification that the blade is stuck. This might have been caused by the edge running into something like a knot or seam if too much dust or debris built up in the cut area or if the blade got into a gouge in the mat from a previous cut. To resume your project, do not unload the mat. This will lose your place in the project, and it will be impossible to get it lined up again. Check the cut area for dust or debris, and gently clean it. If there's dust on top of Clamp B, brush it off with a clean, dry paintbrush. Do not remove the blade. Once the debris is gone, press the Go button. The machine will take a moment to sense the Knife Blade again, and then it will resume cutting.

## Why Is My Fabric Getting Caught Under the Rollers?

Be sure to cut down any fabric so that it fits on your mat without going past the adhesive. If you have stuck the fabric and realize it's hanging past the adhesive, use a ruler and a sharp blade to trim it. Or, if it's the correct size but slightly askew, unstick it and reposition it.

## Why Would My Cricut Maker Continuously Turn Off During Cuts?

This can happen from a build-up of static electricity while cutting foil and metal sheets. Makers in dry areas are more susceptible to this. Spritzing water in the air will dissipate the build-up. Be careful not to spray any water directly on the Maker. Using a vaporizer or humidifier in the area where you use your Maker can help avoid the static build-ups. If this doesn't seem to be what's causing the issue, contact Cricut Member Care.

## What Do I Do About A Failing or Incomplete Firmware Update?

Be sure to use a computer to install the firmware update and that you're connected with a USB cable rather than Bluetooth. Verify that the computer meets the least system requirements; if it doesn't, you'll need to use another computer that does. If it does and you're still having problems, disconnect the Cricut from your computer and turn it off. Restart the computer.

Once it's back on, open Design Space and try the firmware update again. If it still freezes up or doesn't complete, try the update using a different web browser. The subsequent step is to try another USB cable. If that doesn't help or don't have another USB cable to try, contact Cricut Member Care.

## What Do I Do If My Cricut Machine Is Having Power Issues?

If your Cricut Maker, Cricut Explore One, or Cricut Explore Air 2 is having power issues, these are the troubleshooting steps. If the machine doesn't have any control or only has it sometimes, make sure that the plug is completely plugged into the power port on the device, the power adapter, and the wall outlet. The cutting mat can sometimes knock the power cable loose as it goes through the machine. You can evade this by making sure the excess cord isn't bundled up behind the machine. If everything is securely plugged in, make sure that you're using the genuine Cricut power cable that came with your device and that the green light on the adapter is lit up. If you're not using the Cricut power cable, you can buy one or contact Cricut Member Care. If you are, try using a different wall outlet. If it's still having problems, try another Cricut power cable. If the issues continue even after this, take a short video of the issue happening and forward it to Cricut Member Care.

## What Do I Do If I Have Issues with The Machine's Door?

If the door won't open or won't stay open, take a short video to forward on to Cricut Member Care. If the door won't close or won't stay closed, make sure there aren't any accessories loaded into the accessory clamp. If there aren't, take a photo or short video to forward to the Cricut Member Care team.

## Where Can I Download Software for My Cricut Explore Air Machine?

For iOS users or Android users, you can get Cricut Design Space on the iOS App Store and Google Play, respectively. You need to download it, install it and log in

For uses on a computer, visit *design.cricut.com* and then sign in with your login details. There will be a prompt to download Cricut Design Space. Download the plugin and install it and you are good to go.

# TROUBLESHOOTING YOUR CRICUT EXPLORE AIR 2 AND MORE

If your Explore Machine stops working or pauses when you are in the middle of your work, you don't have to worry. Here are some steps in troubleshooting issues.

Is your power button blinking red? If you notice this when you first power the machine or when you are trying to update a framework, that means you have to contact the care center for assistance.

Is the power button light flashing red when trying to load your cutting mat? Then an error might have occurred when saving a corrupted project and that means you will need to recreate the project.

## Your Blade Is Not Detected

STEP 1: Make sure that the tool is properly installed and that the tool matches with the tool recommended by the Design Space. If you don't have access to the recommended tool, return to the project preview screen after which you click on the edit tool to choose a different tool. If the problem persists, then proceed to step 2.

STEP 2: Gently remove the tool again from the clamp and carefully clean the tool sensor with a light cloth. After cleaning, install it back and press the "GO" button.

## Your Machine is Being Unusually Noisy

If the sound of your machine is louder than normal, then check if it is engaged in fast mode for writing or cutting. If checked and it is engaged in fast mode, then you have to contact your care center or proceed to step 2.

STEP 2: Check to ensure that you are making use of the power cord that the machine came with. If you are making use of a different cord, the voltage coming into the Cricut machine may be wrong and may be the cause of the grinding noise. But if you are using the power cord the machine came with and still the machine is making the noise, then proceed to step 3.

STEP 3: Check if the pressure setting you are using is too high and if so, try reducing the pressure setting for the material you are trying to cut.

But if you have tried all these things and it is still not working, please contact the machine care center.

## Your Machine is Tearing Your Material

These are some steps to take if your Cricut machine is tearing your material:

STEP 1: Check if the smart is set on the correct setting and check if you have selected the correct material in the design space.

STEP 2: Try to verify the size and quality of the image you have cut. If you are cutting an image that is of very high quality, try cutting one free from duplicity.

STEP 3: Try making use of a new blade and mat.

STEP 4: After all these steps have been completed and the problem still persists, please try contacting assistance care.

## Your Fabrics Always Get Caught Under the Rollers

If you are experiencing this problem with your fabrics, check if the fabrics are placed outside the tenacious area of your mat by allowing it to pass under the rubber roller bar. If that happens the fabrics can be gripped by the rubber rollers. It is recommended that you cut down a size that will fit the mat but will not extend outside the tenacious area. The recommended and standard sizes for the tenacious area on the fabrics grip mat is 12x24 and 12x12, respectively.

## How to Clean Your Explore Machine

Machines might collect dust, paper, or other particles. Cleaning your machine is very easy to do using the following steps and tips:

- Always make sure your machine is first of all disconnected before cleaning it.
- You can make use of cleaner sprayed on a soft, clean cloth to clean the machine.
- Make sure you clean the electricity panel section with a dry, soft, clean cloth or cotton; or you can simply wipe.

## How to Load Your Paper

When you are using the Cricut Explore Air 2, it is recommended that your paper should be within the 3x3 range as this will help in getting an optimum result for cardstock. However, the Cricut Explore Air 2 is capable of cutting larger paper of 6x12 inches

## Cricut Explore Air 2 Tips

## How to Install Your Cutting Mat

Place the mat into your Cricut machine slowly, make sure that the arrow point towards your device

Click on "load paper" to hold the cutting mat firmly. This will help the loading of the mat into your Cricut Explore machine. If you notice any issues with the loading, then click on "unload" and try processing it again

## How to Remove Your Cut from the Cutting Mat

Slowly remove the cut from your cutting mat. Use the Cricut tool or a craft knife to pull the image or cut. If you are facing any form of difficulty, clean off any paper scrapings remaining on the cutting mat.

## How to Replace Your Cutting Blade

Firstly, remove the cutting blade assembly. After that, release the cutting blade. Slowly remove the blade from the magnet and hold it with care.

To insert a new blade, free the blade release and slowly insert your new blade shaft into the bottom hole of the cutting blade assembly, then reinsert the cutting blade assembly into your Cricut machine.

## How to Apply Grease

Some tips and steps on how to apply grease to your Cricut machine:

- First, turn off the machine.
- Then push the smart carriage gradually to the left.
- Wipe around the entire bar of the cut smart carriage bar with a clean cloth or tissue.
- Push the cut smart carriage slowly to the right.
- Move the cut smart gently to the center of the machine.

- Squeeze a small amount of grease at the end of the cotton swab.
- Apply a little grease on both sides of the cut smart.
- Move gently the cut smart carriage to the left side and also to the right to distribute the grease around.
- Wipe off the grease at the end of the bar.

Review of the Best Cricut Machine for Beginners

Cricut has different models of die-cutting machines and for a beginner, you may be confused about the type that is best for you in the course of crafting. Look no further as I have you covered. I have reviewed four machines (Cricut Maker, Cricut Explore Air 2, Cricut Explore Air, and Cricut Explore One) to give insight into their strengths and weaknesses while making up your mind to which one of them you will work with.

The type of Cricut machine you may wish to get depends on the type of project you want to use it for. All Cricut machines have certain things in common including cut, right, and score, 12" wide cutting area size. They can also cut a variety of materials, as well as the Design Space software and the Print Then Cut feature.

1. Double/Single Tool Holder: the main tool holder is what you see when you open the lid of the Cricut machine, designed to move back and forth on the carriage. A double tool holder allows you to write and cut in one step while a single tool holder will do the same function as separate steps. Among the four mentioned Cricut machines, only Cricut Explore One

has a single tool holder while the rest has a double tool holder.

2. Adaptive Tool System: this is a recent addition to the Cricut machine and available only to Cricut Maker. The adaptive tool system delivers more power to the cutting force (4 kg), which is ten times more than the nearest version to it. It uses a steering system to control the direction of the blade, adjusts the pressure of the blade automatically with each cut pass, and uses a new set of tools and accessories for diverse cuts.

3. Fast Cutting Mode: this mode is used to write and cut materials twice as fast, especially when producing large quantities of materials. This feature is common to Cricut Maker and Explore Air 2.

4. Cutting with Bluetooth: this feature is common to the Cricut Maker, Explore Air 2, and Explore Air. You can use it to cut your material without using a cable.

5. All models of Cricut machines have a slot for cartridge and can be linked to your Design Space account to have access to your cartridge graphics. Newer models like the Cricut Maker come with a digital Design Space library instead of the physical cartridge and if you need to connect a physical cartridge with it, you will need to buy a separate cartridge adapter.

# PROJECT IDEAS FOR YOUR CRICUT EXPLORE AIR 2

## Cutting Letters and Shapes for Scrapbooking

S hapes are one of the most vital features in Cricut Design Space. They are used for creating some of the best designs. In this tutorial, you will learn how to cut letters or texts, how to add shapes and how to adjust the size, colors and rotate shapes.

To add a shape;

1. Log into your Design Space.

2. From the drop-down menu, click "Canvas". You will be taken to the canvas or work area.
3. Click "Shapes" on the left panel of the canvas.
4. A window will pop-up with all the shapes available in Cricut Design Space.
5. Click to add shape.

We have explained the process of adding a shape. To cut a shape;

1. Click "Linetype". Linetype lets your machine know whether you plan on cutting, drawing or scoring a shape.
2. Select "Cut" as Linetype and proceed with cutting the shape.

## Cutting Letters

Cutting letters or texts is simple if you know how to do it. To cut letters;

1. First of all, you need to add the text you want to cut. Click "Add Text" on the left panel of the canvas.
2. Place text in the area where you want to cut it. Highlight text and click on the slice tool. If you have multiple lines of texts, weld them and create a single layer. Then, use the slice tool.
3. Move the sliced letters from the circle and delete the ones you don't need.

# Making Simple Handmade Cards

If you want to test your crafting skills, the Cricut Explore Air 2 has made it possible for you to be creative with designing whatever you want to design on the Design Space. We will be teaching you how to use your Cricut Explore Air 2 to make simple cards.

1. Log into Design Space with your details. Do this on your Mac/Windows PC.
2. On the left-hand side of the screen, select "Shapes". Add the square shape.

3. By default, there is no rectangular shape, so you have to make do with the square shape. However, you can adjust the length and width. You can change the shape by clicking on the padlock icon at the bottom left of the screen. Change the size and click on the padlock icon to relock it.
4. Click "Score Line" and align.
5. Create your first line. It's advisable you make it long. Use the "zoom in" option for better seeing if you are having difficulties with sight.
6. Select the first line you have created and duplicate. It's easier that way than creating another long line. You will see the duplicate option when you right-click on your first line.
7. Follow the same duplication process and create a third line.
8. Rotate the third line to the bottom so that it connects the other two parallel lines you earlier created. Remember to zoom in to actually confirm the lines are touching.
9. Duplicate another line, just like you did the other. Rotate it to the top so that it touches the two vertical parallel lines. You should have created a big rectangular shape.
10. Highlight your rectangular shape (card). Select "Group" at the upper right corner.
11. Now, change the "Score" option "cut". You can do this by clicking on the little pen icon.

12. Your lines will change from dotted to thick straight lines.
13. Select the "Attach" option at the bottom right-hand side of the screen. The four lines will be attached and will get the card ready to be cut on the mat correctly.
14. You can adjust the size of the card as you like. At this point, you can add images or texts beautify your card anyhow you want it.
15. After you are done, select the "Make it" button and then "Continue" to cut your card out.

If you don't know how to create a style on your cards with shapes, follow these simple steps to create one.

1. Select your choice of shape. Let's choose stars for example. Select the "Shape" option and click on the star.
2. Add two stars.
3. Select the first star and click "Flip" and then select "Flip Vertical".
4. Align both stars to overlap them at the center.
5. Select "Weld" to make a new shape and add a score line.
6. Align them at the center and attach them.
7. Select "Make it button" and then "Continue" to cut your card out.

If you don't know how to add text or write on a card, follow the processes below.

1.  Select your choice of shape. Let's choose hexagon for example. Select the "Shape" option and click on the hexagon shape.
2.  Use your favorite pattern.
3.  Add a scoring line and rotate it.
4.  Click "Add Text". A box will appear on the canvas or work area of your project. Write your desired text. Let's say, you choose to write, "A Star Is Born Strong" and "And Rugged" on the two hexagonal shapes. Choose the fonts and style of writing.
5.  Select the first text and flip vertically or horizontally.
6.  Select the second text and flip vertically. Click, "Flip" and select flip vertically. Doing this will make the text not look upside down.
7.  Attach Select "Make it button" and then "Continue" to cut your card out. Follow the cutting process on the screen to full effect.

## Making A Simple T-Shirt

You can use your Cricut Explore Air 2 to make nice T-shirts designs and it's quite easy to do. Cricut cuts out an iron-on vinyl design in an easy and simple way. I will teach you how to make a simple t-shirt with the Cricut Explore Air 2.

In this tutorial, we will be using iron-on vinyl. Iron-on vinyl is a type of vinyl, like an adhesive that will stick to any fabric when applied using an iron.

1.  Log into your Design Space.
2.  Select "New Project" and then, click on "Templates" in the top left corner. Choosing a template makes it easier to visualize your design to know how good or bad it will be on your T-shirt.
3.  Choose "Classic T-Shirt" and pick your preferred style, size, and color.
4.  You will see tons of beautiful designs for iron-on T-shirts. Browse through the entire images before you make your choice.
5.  Remember, if your preferred design isn't available, you can upload your pictures to the Cricut Design Space.

We have created a tutorial on how to upload your own images to Cricut Design Space.

6. After you have selected the image, resize the image to fit the T-shirt. You can do this by clicking the resize handle in the bottom part of your design and dragging the mouse to enlarge or reduce.

7. When you are done, click the "Make it" button in the top right corner. You will be told to connect your Cricut machine.

8. Toggle the green "Mirror" button on. Toggling it on will make sure your design is not cut backward.

9. Face the shiny part of your vinyl design down on your cutting mat. Remember to move the smart set dial to the iron-on option.

10. Remove all the vinyl designs you don't want to be transferred to your project when it's ironed. Use your weeding tool to remove those little bits that will jeopardize your beautiful design. This process is called weeding.

11. Transfer your design to your T-shirt when you are done weeding. You can either use an iron or an EasyPress. Preheat your EasyPress before use.

12. Congrats! You just learned how to make a simple T-shirt on the Cricut Design Space.

# Making A Leather Bracelet

The Cricut Explore Air 2 can be pretty amazing in doing a variety of things. One of those things is being able to make a leather bracelet with your Cricut. You can make pretty cool designs that you can turn to wearable pieces of jewelry.

To make a leather bracelet, you need your Cricut Explore Air 2, a deep point blade, faux leather, marker, ruler, craft knife, bracelet cut file, transfer tape, and a grip mat. You will also need glue, an EasyPress or iron and an SVG design to crown it up.

Follow these steps to create your leather bracelets.

1. Log into your Design Space account menu.

2. Select "Canvas".

3. Upload an art set from Jen Goode into the Design Space. The Jen Goode is a set of designs with 4 different image layouts.

4. Ungroup the designs and hide the layers you don't require after selecting your design.

5. Create a base cut of the shape you want to use. Use a cut file and create the shape you want. For example, you can use a shape tool to create a circular design.

6. Add circle cutouts with basic shapes. Duplicate the layer so, that you will use it for the back of the bracelet.

7. Set your iron or EasyPress ready and apply the vinyl to the uppermost layer of your leather.

8. Spread a thin coat of glue on the back of the duplicated layer and press it with the other layer together.

9. Add your bracelet strap or chain together with some other ornaments.

10. Congratulations! You have just made your first leather bracelet.

## Making a Stencil for Painting with The Cricut Explore Air 2

To make a stencil, you can either use the ready-made designs or make your own design. This tutorial will be based on how to create a stencil for painting.

1. Log in to your Design Space.
2. Click "Canvas" from the drop-down menu.
3. Click "Add Text".
4. Highlight text and change to your preferred font.
5. All your letters must be separated. If they aren't, click the ungroup button to separate. The letters must overlap. This will allow you to drag each letter as you please.
6. Arrange your text line as you want it. If you notice each letter is still showing individually, highlight the text box and click "Weld" at the bottom right of the panel.
7. Click "Attach". Make sure the text is highlighted. This will make the letters arranged properly when it goes to the cut mat.
8. Your stencil design is ready!

# Making a Vinyl Sticker

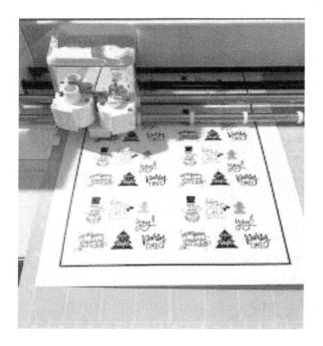

First of all, you need to have an idea of the vinyl sticker that you want. Get ideas online or from forums. Once you have gotten the picture, make a sketch if it to see how the sticker would look. After you have done this, follow the steps below;

1. Use an image editing software like Photoshop or Illustrator. Design to your taste and save. Make sure you know the folder it is saved to.
2. Now, open your Design Space.
3. Click "New Project".
4. Scroll to the bottom left-hand side and click "Upload".
5. Drag and drop the design you created with your photo editing app.

6. Select your image type. If you want to keep your design simple, select simple.

7. Select which area of the image that is not part of it.

8. Before you forge ahead, select the image as cut to have a preview. You can go back if there is a need for adjustments.

9. Select "Cut".

10. Weed excess vinyl.

11. Use a transfer tape on top of the vinyl. This will make the vinyl stay in position.

12. Go over the tape and ensure all the bibles are nowhere to be found.

13. Peel away the transfer tape and you have your vinyl sticker.

# MAKING MONEY WITH YOUR CRICUT EXPLORE AIR 2

## Initial Things to Keep in Mind

- *Be different:* Be yourself. Try to be creative and unique.
- *Keep it narrow*: You might feel that making and selling everything under the sun gives you more variety, customers, and hence more money. It doesn't work that way. Strive to be an expert and the best there is in the craft you choose. Decide what area of craftiness you want to be known for.
- *Be consistent*: You won't get far if you choose to ignore your business for weeks or months.
- *Sell quality products*: People will pay for quality over quantity and recommend you to their friends.

## Business Ideas You Can Make and Sell with Your Cricut

As it turns out, the smaller the craft, the more profitable it ends up being. Less shipping costs, less material, and everything works out.

- *Vinyl Crafts*: vinyl is a perfect crafting material. It is relatively cheap, lightweight, and easy to ship. Most importantly, there is so much you can do with this material.

- *Wall Art*: There are over a million searches on Pin-interest for farmhouse wall art. Don't get left out on the actions.
- *Customized Decals*: Customized stickers are perfect because they are used for so many parties and home decor.
- *Kids Related Wall Decals*: Kids related decorations happen all year round and there is a never-ending need for baby and kids' decor.
- *Stickers*: Alike in vein to vinyl decals, stickers are hot items for the reason that of the customization potentials and their low shipping costs.
- *Wedding Decorations and Souvenirs*: Wedding Decors and Souvenirs are one of the bestselling Cricut projects. The wedding industry is alive and this is no surprise. The search for backyard weddings has gone up by 441% according to Pin-interest.
- *Paper Flowers*: Just like farmhouse decorations, paper flowers are popular with over a million searches for it every month. They are great for every event from Weddings to Mother's Day to Baby Showers.

## How to Save Money While Using Your Cricut Explore Air 2 Machine for Business

- *Clean your Mats and Reuse them*: If you fail to clean and re-stick your old mats, you definitely should! However, if your mat losses it's sticking power, try using some adhesive spray. Make sure the mat surface is neat and tape the boundaries so they do not become sticky. Seize your spray then cover the mat surface. It should be good as new.

- *Keep Vinyl on a Roll*: As an alternative of cutting off a novel quantity of vinyl each time you cut out a new design, attempt leaving your vinyl on the roll. In that method, when you are through cutting, you can use some scissors to cut around the used section. This will save you from wasting precious vinyl.

- *Order in Bulk*: If you own a vinyl cutting business, your main expenses are likely blanks and vinyl. Try ordering in bulk and in wholesale. Most stores will give you a good discount for doing this, so there is a ton of money to be saved.

- *Use free SVG files and fonts:* A lot of websites and designers offer you these files and fonts for free. Most of these items are for personal use and would require you to purchase a license before you can sell any item made using the design. However, some are free for commercial use!

- *Check the energy consumption of you heat press:* The rate at which the easy press consumes electricity is something most people don't consider when buying a heat press! Heat presses are an industrial appliance and they consume a lot of power. Most heat press does not come with an in-built auto shut-off timer which consumes much electricity if you fail to turn it off. Make sure to consider this if you are currently in the market for a new heat press! I recommend using Easy Press 2.

# Vinyl Tricks

- Painting a coating of mod podge onto a canvas every time you are adding vinyl makes it stick. Not undertaking it roots a lot of stress and hindrance and about an additional hour of trying to get it to adhere to the canvas.
- When making a stencil, paint a layer of mod podge over the stencil to seal the edges so that only the mod podge bleeds and it dries clear!
- Use silhouette transfer tape. It works like magic and saves you a lot of headaches.
- First, use alcohol to clean off all-ceramic and glass projects. It helps the vinyl stick!
- Ensure you mirror all heat transfer projects! You want the project to be backward after you cut it out.
- If you are doing a layered project, add boxes at top of your design so you can easily line up the layers.
- Make sure your design is inside the cut lines in your software. If the image is large, your blade won't cut the entire design and it will waste your vinyl.
- Always make sure the shiny side of your vinyl is down when you load it into your machine.

## Cricut Transfer Tapes

Cricut transfer tapes are designed specifically to make the transfer of vinyl designs to project surfaces very easy. The clear grid film allows you to easily fix the design right on the material. Choosing the right tape is easy:

- *Transfer Tape*: Transfer tapes are used with most vinyl types, particularly those with a smooth, non-textured finish.
- *StrongGrip Transfer Tape*: These tapes are used on vinyl with a textured finish such as Shimmer, Glitter, and True Brushed Vinyl. This tape is hard and should not be used on other vinyl types.

Apply Transfer Tape

- Peel the liner from the Transfer Tape and attach a little bit of the tape to your design either at the center or at one corner of the design.
- Use a Scraper to externally polish the tape onto your design from the area where you added the tape.
- Turn the vinyl over and polish the backside.

Apply to Project surface

- Ensure the surface of the project is clean and dry. Clean the plastic and glass surfaces with rubbing alcohol.
- Peel liner from the tape and design.
- If the vinyl is not separated from the liner, simply polish liner back onto the vinyl and peel away again.
- Add a little bit of the design, either at the center or end onto the surface
- Use a Scraper to outwardly polish the tape onto your design from the area where you added the tape.

- Peel away the transfer tape from the design.
- Always be cautious. If the vinyl peels off with the tape, simply polish the tape and vinyl back to the surface of the project and peel it off again.

## Best Piece of Vinyl to Use for Your Projects

There are two main types of vinyl (Adhesive and Heat Transfer Vinyl.). There are varieties of styles and types within each of these two categories.

Adhesive vinyl (sticker vinyl) is a flexible, pressure-sensitive adhesive material that can be used for any design and used on any kind of surface. They come in various colors and finishes, but they always come with a paper backing and it is sticky when the paper backing has been shed off.

Heat transfer vinyl is similar to the heat-activated adhesive material designed for use on all kinds of fabric surfaces or any heat-resistant surface. Both vinyl types are available in rolls or sheets, usually 12″ wide. Heat transfer vinyl has a clear plastic sheet used to cover the vinyl. The back side of the vinyl is the adhesive side which is not sticky and it is the part where you will make your cuts.

Type of Adhesive Vinyl you can use

There are few adhesive vinyl's which is meant for lasting outdoor use while some are made to be temporal for indoor use.

- *Permanent outdoor vinyl:* These are perfect for car decals, outdoor signs, mugs, and other items that are washed using the dishwasher.
- *Removable indoor vinyl:* These are perfect for indoor signs, wall decals, stencils, and whenever you need temporary applications

Varieties of Adhesive Vinyl

- Stencil Vinyl
- Etched Glass Vinyl
- Glitter Vinyl
- Metallic Vinyl
- Patterned Vinyl
- Chalkboard Vinyl
- Glow in the Dark Vinyl

Varieties of Heat Transfer Vinyl

- *Siser Easyweed:* it is very easy to use. It comes in different kinds of colors, washes and wears well.
- *Flocked HTV:* This has a soft texture, simple to weed, and is recommended for beginners.
- Glitter HTV
- Metallic HTV
- Holographic HTV
- Reflective HTV
- Stretch HTV
- Patterned HTV

However, several vinyl types work better for various kinds of materials and designs. For instance, holographic in addition metallic vinyl are often more rigid and work best on designs with tiny pieces of vinyl. The stretch vinyl works best with flexible knit, athletic or ribbed fabrics. All HTV can be washed, but following instructions will help your finished piece to stay good for longer.

# MORE PROJECT IDEAS

## Custom Transparent Pouch

The necessary equipment:

- A transparent pouch
- Peach and mint colored vinyl
- A cutting machine with a fine-tipped blade

Custom pouch tutorial:

First, you can cut a sufficiently large strip into 2 vinyl rolls to prepare the cut. You can then use the cutting mat "Light Grip" to position the vinyl (one after the other, following the software). The vinyl is laid with the colored part up. The Cricut will cut the different elements by itself:

It is then necessary to peel off the carpet's vinyl, which can be done very quickly. Then, each element must be detached and carefully glued to the pouch. Then, you can rule to try to align the patterns by lines. But you can, of course, choose the distribution you want! By the way, you can decorate only one side, but it is quite possible to do both.

And then, we have the custom kit. It can be used as a kit to store your stationery or all those small items you tend to lose when doing crafts. Peach motifs make it almost a full-fledged decorative object. But for those who leave this summer and have planned to go to the beach or the pool, this pouch can be used to store their swimsuit, sunglasses, sunscreen... it can also simply serve as a toiletry bag or makeup.

## The Card "Ice"

The necessary equipment:

- 4 sheets of cardstock (Depending on the colors you want)
- A glue sticks
- A cutting machine with a fine-tipped blade

Achievement:

To make this, you don't have to make things hard for yourself: Place at each step a sheet of cardboard paper on the cutting mat and start the machine.

Then just paste the whole thing. The white part serves as a "support"; it is also on its back that one can write the card's contents. It is necessary to glue the pale pink paper, then the dark pink, and finally the yellow banner and the writing "ice cream". I told you: it's all simple.

Again, think of the several uses for this handmade card. Of course, we can write on it and send it to whoever we want. The idea of matching through postcards personally pleases me always as much. But this card can also be merely decorative, put on a desk, a shelf, or even placed in a moodboard for the summer.

## Simple Cloth Napkins

Now, let's learn how to create our customized cloth napkin with the Cricut Explore Air 2. It is a good idea for those who want to do a quick project to take advantage of scraps and incidentally put our grain of sand in the sustainability of the planet.

The other day, like every morning, I was done with breakfast, and I took a paper napkin to press my lips to it and remove excess stain.

I had never stopped to think about the number of napkins that I threw away with that simple gesture, but when I was aware of it, I set out to create a reusable fabric version, and that is what here I am going to teach you to do with the Cricut machine.

**For this project, you will need:**

- Scraps of cotton fabric.
- Adhesive textile vinyl (optional)

**How to get it done**

1. The first step will be to cut two rectangles of fabric 14 cm long x 11 cm wide with the Cricut machine.
2. When you have the pieces cut, place one on top of the other with the rights facing each other and, with a seam allowance of 1cm, sew around it, leaving an open space to turn the piece over.
3. Now, flip it over, so the right side of the fabric is facing out, iron the piece, and backstitch around near the fabric's edge.

Now comes the creative part.

4. We are going to cut a textile vinyl with the Cricut machine to decorate our art strand.
5. Search the internet for an image that you like and save it on your computer.
6. Next, log into the Cricut Design Space platform, start a new project, and upload the downloaded image. Depending on the image, you should choose the most appropriate option (Simple, medium complexity, or complex).
7. If your image has a background that you want to delete, you will have to do it in the next window; if it does not have experience (a checkerboard will appear), click to continue.
8. In the next window, select the option "Save as cut image" and fill in the project name and tags to make it easier to search.
9. You will have the image ready to cut it into vinyl using the corresponding mat for it.
10. Now you just have to iron it in the desired place according to the manufacturer's instructions, and you will have finished this beautiful and practical makeup accessory.

You can sew on several and wash them by hand each time you use it, or you can pile them up and then put them in the washing machine!

# Explosive Box: How to Make Halloween Souvenir

Trick or treat? This is the phrase that we hear the most in Halloween films, especially in comedy and children's movies. However, although we always think about sweets, the story of Halloween is a little more frightening.

Explosive Box: Halloween Souvenir - Box Materials

Preparing this explosive box is very easy; besides, you will need a few materials for this. You can even call the kids to help. Look at the material you will need:

- Cricut Explore Air 2
- Cricut Spatula
- Color Plus Paper 180g A4 size BLACK

- Color Plus Paper 180g size A4 ORANGE CARTAGENA
- Color Plus Paper 180g A4 size GREEN BUENOS AIRES
- Color Plus Paper 180g A4 size
- Color Plus Paper Opaline 180g
- Cricut Red Pen
- Glue
- You'll also have to download the Free File for the Explosive Halloween Boxes

**Tutorial**

1. To start, open the file in Cricut's Design Space program and adjust it to the indicated size 50x35cm (it is marked at the top of the border surrounding the file).
2. Now, switch the internal lines to POINTING mode. This way, they will be creased and not cut.
3. However, to achieve the "blood in the eyes" effect, change the inner lines of the white part of the eye to DRAW mode.
4. Now it's time to cut. Let's start with the eyes with the effect of "blood in the eyes". Fit the Cricut Pen to the holder. To do this, press gently until you hear the CLICK!

So then, Cricut makes the drawings and then the cut! A maximum advantage, right? Yea, I know!!!

5. After the drawing is done, replace the pen with the crease tool, as we will start cutting the box!

6.  Cut and Crease at Cricut

Anyway, with all the pieces cut, it's time to assemble. And I'm going to warn you: It's so easy to do! Now is the time to call the kids to participate!

7.  Let's start by gluing the seam part to complete the box. After that, just double it!
8.  Fold in the creased part of the box. At the bottom (at the base of the box), we do not glue anything else! Since this is what will give the explosion effect when we remove the cap!
9.  After that, fold the lid part and glue the sides.
10. Attach the lid to the box to start decorating. It is essential to fit to see how high the eyes will be.
11. Creed! That bloody eye is scary! Let's put it in place!
12. Glue your eyes and mouth ...
13. Ehmm!!! But something seems to be missing? Do you know it?
14. Of course! The screws! Have you seen Frankenstein without a screw? Fold and glue the screw parts!
15. Then, just join these two parts!
16. Glue the screws to the cover! And ready!!!!

Just see how easy it is to make this explosive Frankenstein box. It is ready to be filled with treats. The only certainty is that the kids will love it.

# Pumpkin Box and Ghost Box

However, you may be wondering how to make the other boxes. The process is the same. However, in the explosive pumpkin box, you will use the Color Plus Cartagena paper, the orange color, to make the lid and the body. Therefore, the Color Plus Los Angeles paper, black, will only be used for the eyes, nose, and mouth.

In the same way, you make the ghost! However, in it, you will use Opalina paper for the cover and body and black for the eyes and mouth.

Now we have a thrilling trio! Trick or treat?

## Custom Pillows

Personalized pillows can be the highlight of a decoration. Therefore, know how to choose the fabric's color and transfer it to be used in production.

To make this pillow, you will need:

- Cricut Explore Air 2
- Light or Standard cutting base
- Easy Press + application base or iron
- Bright Pad
- Sewing machine

- Cricut circular cutter and fabric scissors
- Cricut Hook
- Regenerative cutting base
- Ruler
- Transfer to Cricut fabric
- Printed and white fabric 100% cotton
- Pompom or other finish - or nothing if you prefer!
- Padding
- Pins, clips, and sewing thread

For many, one burning question begging for answers when completing their craft is:

Can I use my iron instead of Easy Press?

Of course, you can. The whole point here is the efficiency of the equipment. Unlike iron, Easy Press was created for this job, so it applies the transfer perfectly.

How to get it done

The first part of every project is the art or design that will be cut. So, the most certain thing is to start with that part. Most people prefer to use an already saved image file. All that is left is to fixate them inside the Design Space to cut.

How to Open Image in Design Space

With the program open, click Upload and choose an image to upload to the program.

Right after that, you will define what type of image you are uploading. You can choose between Simple (for flat core images), Moderately Complex (with more details and various colors), and Complex (with gradients and textures).

Click Continue, and on the next screen, you will be able to make some edits such as deleting the background of the image or even some part of the drawing. When you're the way you want, just save.

Now open this image in Canvas and start by defining the size of the image you will crop. To do this, select all parts of your image and group to work all at once safely.

To define the size, you can use the blue circle in the lower right corner of the image selection box or place the tool's measurements on the top bar.

# CRICUT DESIGN SPACE

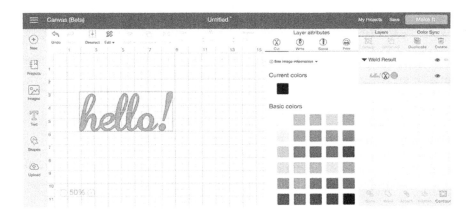

T he Cricut Mini was one of the first machines that worked with a computer. The design software it used was called Cricut Craft Room. Cricut Craft Room was the predecessor of Design Space. With the advancement in technology, the Cricut cutting machines also became more advanced. As the Cricut machines advanced, the design software needed to keep up with them. Cricut Craft Room was slowly phased out in 2018, and Design Space became the design software that is currently used with Cricut cutting machines.

With Design Space, there are unlimited possibilities. Depending on the cutting machine, some of the older design cartridges can still be used with the software. Design Space has a library full of preloaded designs, templates, and images. You are not limited to using Design Space or Cricut images either. You can also upload your own images.

# Getting Started with Cricut Design Space

Once you have downloaded Design Space, you will find it easy to learn the program. Design Space costs nothing to download and install. Although there are some designs, images, and fonts that are charged to your account, there are many free images, templates, shapes, and fonts.

Once you have a Design Space ID, you have access to the software's vast library of designs and all of its cutting capabilities. Design Space offers a limited time free trial of Cricut Access, which is a membership-based library of images, designs, projects, and more.

The great thing about Design Space is that you do not have to have a Cricut Access membership to buy any of the projects, images, or designs. You can purchase them if and when you require them.

## Cricut Design Space Quick Guide

## Design Space Screens

There are two main screens for Design Space.

## Home Screen

This is the first screen you will encounter when Design Space loads. You can click on any of the project windows in each section to access or view the projects.

The screen is split into the following sections:

*Top Menu Bar* — This is the top, dark gray Menu bar. It is when you are on the Home screen, this menu bar will have the following options on it:

- Home — This indicates the screen you are viewing.
- Welcome <Name> message — This will have your login name.
- My Projects — This will take you to the directory of your stored/saved projects.
- Machine — This is the cutting machine selection menu. The minute you have selected your default machine, the machine will be loaded every time you log in.
- "New Project" button — This will send you to a clean Canvas screen to begin working on a new project.

*My Projects* — This will list all of your current projects.

*Cricut Access* — This will list the latest ready-to-make projects from Cricut Access.

*My Ready-to-Make Projects* — This section selects ready-to-make projects for you, based on your latest projects.

*Other promotional sections* — There are a few sections that display the latest projects and materials available to you.

## Canvas Screen

This is the Design Screen where you will create all of your projects.

The Canvas screen is split into the following sections:

*Top Menu Bar* — This is the top, dark gray Menu bar. When you are on the Canvas screen, this menu bar will have the following options on it:

- Canvas — This indicates the screen you are viewing.
- Untitled — This will remain "Untitled" until you have saved your current project. If you load a saved project, it will list the name of the opened project.
- My Projects — This will take you to the directory of your stored/saved projects.
- Save — This is the save button for your project. Once a project has been saved, there will be a second option listed "Save As". The "Save As" option is there so you can save a project as another name and keep the current one intact.
- Machine — This is the cutting machine selection menu. Once you have selected your default machine, it will load every time you log in.

"Make it" button — This button sends your current project to the "Prepare" screen to ready your design for cutting.

*Top Drop-down Menu Bar* (3 stripes in the top left-hand corner of the gray menu bar)

*The Design Panel* — This is the selection panel on the left-hand side of the screen. Sometimes, it is simply called the left-hand menu. The Design Panel is where you can select the object you are going to use for your design projects. These objects include

Templates, Projects, Images, Text, Shapes, and an option to upload your own designs.

*Edit Menu* — This menu can be found below the top gray menu bar. It should be noted that this menu bar can change slightly depending on the object being designed. Some of the common features of this menu are:

*Undo/Redo option* — The first items on the left of the Edit menu are the Undo and Redo arrows. They are grayed out until there is an object on the screen or until an object has been changed. This is handy when you accidentally move, delete, or resize something on the screen.

*Linetype* — This is where the image or design linetype is determined. The default is always set to "Cut". The "Draw" option is for use with the Cricut Ink Pen accessories. The "Score Line" option is for marking a fold in the material.

*The Linetype Color Swatch block* — This is the small square next to the Linetype options. This option is used to determine what the color of the line will be.

*Fill* — The Fill option is used to change the color of the object on the screen. It is also where you will set the object to "Print". These are for features called "Print" and "Cut". This is when you send an image to the inkjet printer before cutting the material. It is for when you have various shapes, images, or objects that need to be drawn before they are cut.

*The Fill Color Swatch block* — This change the fill color of the chosen object on the screen.

*Select* — This option will "Select All" images on the screen. Once the images have been selected, this option changes to "Deselect"

*Edit* — This is the standard editing menu that contains the "Cut", "Copy", and "Paste" options.

*Align* — This option aligns selected images either horizontally or vertically, or centers them. It also contains a "Distribute" option, which equally spaces out images either vertically or horizontally.

*Arrange* — This arranges the order of the objects.

*Flip* — This "Flips" the object either vertically or horizontally. It also rotates it by 90°.

*Size* — This option resizes the selected image(s).

*Rotate* — This option allows you to rotate objects to a certain angle. It allows for some interesting object positioning on the screen.

*Position* — This will place a selected object at the desired coordinates.

*The Layers and Color Sync panel* — This is the panel found on the right-hand-side of the Canvas screen. It is broken into two tabs.

*Layers tab* — The layers tab has a menu with the following options at the top:

- *Group* — Objects that need to be kept together on the screen to be moved, marked, colored, etc. are easier to work with when they are grouped.
- *Ungroup* — Ungroup is grayed out until objects have been grouped. Ungroup disconnects Grouped objects.
- *Duplicate* — This option is used to clone selected objects and make an exact replica of them.
- *Delete* — This option is used to delete selected objects.

*Color Sync tab* — This tab is useful when you have objects that you want to be drawn or printed in the exact same color. It will list the exact colors of all the objects on the screen for you to match other objects with.

*Canvas Objects* — The panel beneath the Layers panel menu lists all the objects currently on the design screen. As you get more familiar with working in Design Space, you will find this panel very useful.

*Bottom Menu of the Layers/Color Sync panel* — The bottom section of this panel has the following options:

*Canvas* — This hide or unhides any embedded objects on the Canvas, such as templates or background color.

*Slice* — This is for slicing up an object on the canvas.

*Weld* — Welds two objects together to form an outline.

*Attach* — Attaches objects on the screen that need to be printed together.

*Flatten* — Flattens an image with multiple parts into a single image.

*The Design Canvas* — This is the graphed space in the middle of the screen where you will do all of your designs. It is set in inches as a default, but the settings can be customized through the top right-hand Drop-down menu.

At the bottom right-hand corner of the Canvas is the *Zoom Control*. This is grayed out until you hover the mouse cursor over it. By default, it is set to 100% scale. You can set it to zoom in or out of the screen by using the + and - selection icons on each side of the current zoom % marker.

## Prepare Screen

This is a screen that you will get to when you are ready to start cutting the project and have pressed the "Make it" button.

Top Gray Menu — The Drop-down menu on the left of this menu only has one option when you are at the "Prepare" screen, that is to take you back to the Canvas. The name of the menu changes to "Prepare", and next to the name you will see the number of machine mat changes the project requires (1 mat). There will be the name of the project and the name of the cutting machine.

The left-hand panel has the following options:

*Project copies* — This must not be confused with the number of cuts. This option will duplicate the design objects according to the amount selected.

*Small Mat image* — Depending on the number of machine mats required for the project, you could see a number of these small mats. This is where you select the mat you want to edit, rearrange, etc. Next to the mat, it will tell you if the machine is going to cut or draw the object. It may also indicate if the object is to be printed.

*Material Size* — Here you can select the material size. This helps to cut down on using unnecessary material.

*Mirror* — The sliding button next to this option will turn mirroring on or off. Mirroring turns the objects on the mat's upside down.

*Machine Mats* — In the middle of the screen, you will find an exact replica of the machine mat and how the design is placed to be cut. You can move objects around the screen to position them for cutting.

*Cancel button* — In the bottom right-hand corner of the screen, you will find the "Cancel" button. This button will cancel the cut and return you to the Design Canvas screen.

*Continue button* — In the bottom right-hand corner of the screen is the "Continue" button. This takes the cutting to the next stage. You will be prompted to load the accessories in the cutting machine, select the material being used, and load the machine mat.

## Menu Bars

There are two main menu bars that the Home screen, Canvas, and Prepare screens have in common. These menus are:

## Top Menu Bar

This is the dark gray menu bar that changes slightly depending on the screen you are in.

## Top Drop-Down Menu Bar

Next to the screen name on the gray menu bar there are three horizontal lines. These lines represent a drop-down menu. This menu is the same for the Home screen and the Canvas screen. The Prepare screen is slightly different (see the Prepare screen for details). The Drop-down menu options are as follows.

# CONCLUSION

A big thanks again for downloading this book, CRICUT EXPLORE AIR 2.

I hope that this book had helped you understand how to use your Cricut Explore Air 2.

Here is a summary of what to do when using your Cricut Explore Air 2:

1.  Decide on a design
2.  Download the Design Space app
3.  Design your project using the Design Space app
4.  Order a fabric cutting mat (if you don't have one already)
5.  Go to www.cricutexpressions.com and download the Cricut Air app for free. You don't have to create an account, just download it and use it offline without connecting to Wi-Fi or data.
6.  Plug in your Cricut Explore Air 2 and let it charge for at least 2 hours before you begin using it for the first time unless you bought an extra adapter to plug into a wall socket so that it can charge while plugged in running when you start working with your Cricut Explore Air 2.
7.  Follow the instructions on the machine itself to turn it on.
8.  Start designing your project using the Design Space app. You can only use the Design Space app if you

have a Wi-Fi connection or data service on your phone/tablet/laptop or computer that you're using to design with. Once your design is done, save it and then get ready to upload it onto your Cricut Explore Air 2 machine. If you don't want to be using this machine's touchscreen, go into settings and select "Use Cricut Explore Air 2 Controls".

9. Open the Cricut Air app and select "Upload Tool" at the lower right of the screen next to where it says "Cricut Maker by Provo Craft". Select your saved .c2s design file from wherever you saved it onto your laptop/phone/tablet's memory or computer's hard drive, so that you can upload it onto your Cricut Explore Air 2 machine by tapping "Preview & Order" once you've selected the .c2s file in step 10 below.

10. After selecting "Preview & Order", tap "Have a Print Ready File". Select the images on the album you want to use and then tap "Choose" at the bottom of the screen. Then locate your Cricut Explore Air 2 in your craft room (if you're using its touchscreen), hold down on its green power button for 2-3 seconds until it says "Plugged In! Tap to Start", then wait for it to fully charge for at least 2 hours before you begin using it. Make sure that its USB cord is connected properly into a powered USB port on either the Cricut Explore Air 2's main board or wherever you're using its USB cord for your computer, so that everything can communicate and move properly between them.

11. After your Cricut Explore Air 2 has fully charged for at least two hours, open up the Design Space app again and choose "Add New Project" from under "Projects" in that same lower right section of the screen like before like shown below:

12. After selecting "Add New Project", tap anywhere that has a red circle with an exclamation point around it under any project boxes that have already been created by other users or found when browsing projects online. If no red circles with an exclamation point are found, just click anywhere to the left of the "New Project" box until one appears and then type your Cricut Explore Air 2's model number into that box. Then tap "Add New Project."

13. After adding your first project, wait for those screens with the design in them to load using a progress bar at the bottom of the screen as shown below. Once it has finished loading, you have access to all of your projects from wherever you were on Step #10 above:

14. To view all of your projects that are uploaded onto your Cricut Explore Air 2 and ready for you to download and print, tap the "Projects" tab from anywhere on the main page.

15. To save an image onto your computer for later use and reuse in another project, download it from wherever you saved it onto their memory or hard drive:

    1. To open up a . bmp file on your computer and edit it on your computer:

16. To take/edit/make an image from scratch, tap the "Image Editor" tab from anywhere on the entire page or anywhere else that has a blue tab over it at the top:

17. Scroll through your projects' images and tap any of them you'd like to play or edit with your Cricut Explore Air 2 to add new layers within the project's design or undo previous ones. Tap the image at the top of all images within a project to select all of them (but not necessarily all of them at once, just those displayed in between saved files) then tap "Add", "Remove", or "Reverse" from the bottom above each image's preview thumbnail to edit each one in turn until you have what you want inside of that particular project:

18. To preview and print any projects on your Cricut Explore Air 2, tap the "Printing" tab from anywhere on the main page or anywhere else that has a blue tab over it at the top like this:

19. The designs are saved and stored onto your Cricut Explore Air 2's main board for you to print as many times as you'd like using a printing system.

That will be all for now. Enjoy and do not be afraid to experiment.

Made in United States
Orlando, FL
26 March 2023

31447889R00068